These studies have been designed to aid in the development
and maintenance of the ability to sight read on the guitar.

To receive maximum benefit from them you should observe
the following: First, set and maintain a reasonable tempo
for each study...speed is unimportant. Second, DO NOT STOP
(for any reason) before the completion of the study.
(Example; even if you play every note of measure 4
incorrectly, get the first note of measure 5...right, and
on time.) Last (and certainly not least) DO NOT practice
any study until it approaches memorization. This will
completely defeat the purpose of this book. Keep moving on
through the studies even though some have been played
poorly...and when you have reached the point of total
failure, go back to the beginning and start again. Each
time through, you will progress a little farther.

Good Luck

Wm. G. Leavitt

FIRST (OR OPEN) POSITION SCALES AND FINGERINGS

Chromatic Scale   (Play as single lines, NOT as octaves)

C major   A minor   (Relative Harmonic Minor)

F major   D minor

G major   E minor

Bb major   G minor

D major   B minor

Eb major   C minor

A major   F# minor

Ab major   F minor

2

E major  **C# minor**

Db major  **Bb minor**

B major  **G# minor**

Gb major 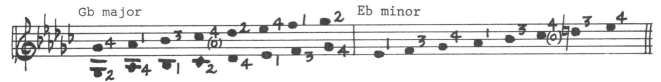 **Eb minor**

F# major

Cb major  **Ab minor**

C# major

Whole tone

Diminished

I

4

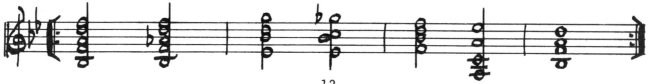

12

E major   C# minor

Db major   Bb minor

B major   G# minor

Gb major   Eb minor

F# major

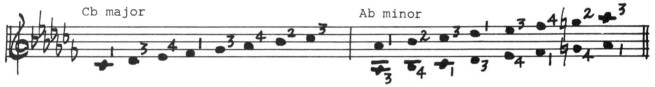

Cb major   Ab minor

C# major

Whole tone

Diminished

15

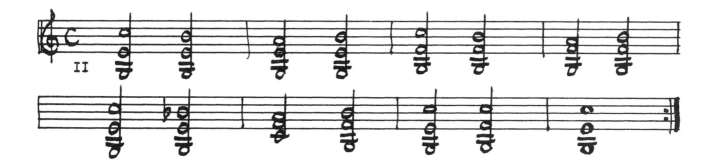

II

II

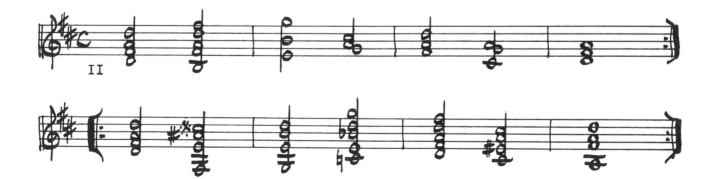

23

29

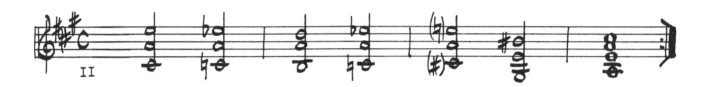

30

31

Chromatic, Whole Tone and Diminished scales have been omitted, as they are identical in all (closed) positions.

E major — C# minor

Db major — Bb minor

B major — G# minor

Gb major — Eb minor

F# major

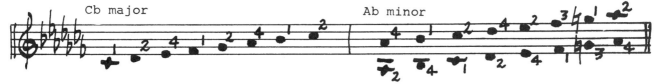

Cb major — Ab minor

C# major

In view of the fact that all scales and closed position
(movable) fingerings have been shown in positions II and III;
(Easy and difficult fingerings in easy and difficult keys)
no more pages such as these will appear in this book. It is
up to the student to learn these patterns well enough to
be able to function in all keys over the rest of the fingerboard.
.... Remember: Same key, new position = new pattern.

III

III

III

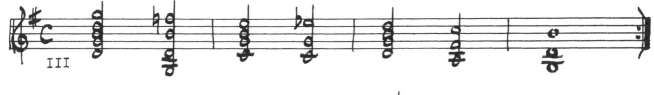

III

III

rit.   atempo

rit.

III

III

III

III

III

III

III

III

III

III

IV

play ♪♫ as ♪³♪

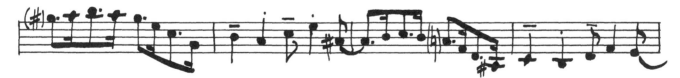

56

IV

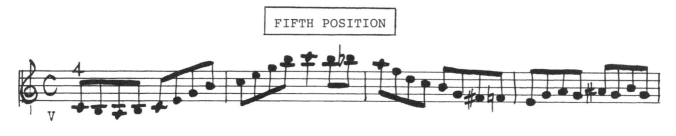

V

(fine)

D.C. al fine

Rit —

V

73

75

VI

VI

VI

VI

VI

90

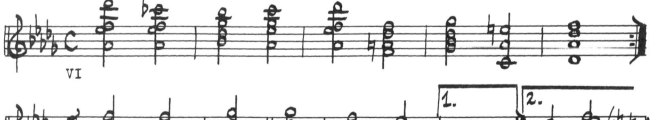

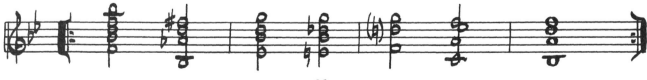

91

VI

VI

93

94

VII

Rit.____   A Tempo

Rit ____

VII

95

VII

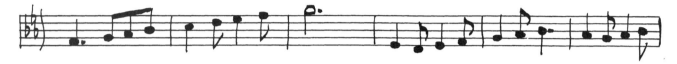

VII

VII

VII

Rit.—

VII

VII

Rit.

A Tempo

Rit.

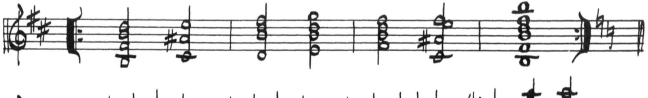